9/2208767

ENOUGH
IS PLENTY

THE YEAR ON THE DINGLE PENINSULA

FELICITY HAYES-MCCOY from Dublin has had a successful career as a writer, working in theatre, radio, television and digital media. She shares an interest in design, folklore and the Irish language with her husband, English opera director Wilf Judd. In 2002, they bought and restored a house in Corca Dhuibhne, Ireland's Dingle peninsula. They now live and work there and in Bermondsey, London. Her published works include stories for children and her memoir, *The House on an Irish Hillside*.

For more information, visit www.felicityhayesmccoy.co.uk
You can also keep up to date at
https://www.facebook.com/fhayesmccoy

To Alice Judd who became Pat Fisher

ENOUGH IS PLENTY

THE YEAR ON THE DINGLE PENINSULA

Felicity Hayes-McCoy

The Collins Press

FIRST PUBLISHED IN 2015 BY
The Collins Press
West Link Park
Doughcloyne
Wilton
Cork

Photographs courtesy Felicity Hayes-McCoy and Wilf Judd,
except for pp. 150 and 151, which are courtesy Isabel Bennett.

A CIP record for this book is available from the British Library.

Hardback ISBN: 978-1-84889-236-1
PDF eBook ISBN: 978-184889-889-9
EPUB eBook ISBN: 978-184889-890-5
Kindle ISBN: 978-184889-891-2

Design and typesetting by Dennison Design
Typeset in Gill Sans & Baskerville
Printed in Malta by Gutenberg Press Limited

Contents

Foreword

When I finished Felicity Hayes-McCoy's first book, *The House on an Irish Hillside*, I felt a sense of well-being. I had walked with her around the peninsula and experienced her wonder and delight. The book glowed with an appreciation of her lifestyle in Dingle.

When I began her second book, *Enough is Plenty*, I wondered if the magic would continue. It did! I was again immersed in her warm appreciation of this mystical place and delighted to revisit Nellie's house and again meet Felicity's husband Wilf and good neighbour Jack. In her second book she has settled into life in Dingle and the fruits of her garden are finding their way on to her kitchen table. Wonderful pictures capture the wildness of the Dingle peninsula and recipes accompany the pictures of her home-grown produce. She digs deeper into the significance of ancient Celtic rituals and the traces of their influence on the present-day life in Dingle, lacing the old to the new.

This book is a celebration of all that is good and meaningful in Dingle, in Kerry and, indeed, in Ireland.

Alice Taylor

Introduction

This is a book about ordinary things and small, bright pleasures that can easily go unnoticed.

It's a view of the year from a stone house on Ireland's Dingle peninsula, a place where life is still marked and shaped by Ireland's Celtic past. People who live here still use the Irish language in their everyday life. In Irish, the peninsula is called Corca Dhuibhne which is pronounced something like 'Korka Gweena'. That name itself holds an ancient memory. It means 'the territory of the people of the Goddess Danú', a fertility goddess worshipped under many names in different lands across millennia.

For the ancient Celts, darkness, however bleak, barren or long drawn out, contains by its nature the dormant seeds of light. It's a belief reflected in the Celtic calendar which sees winter, not springtime, as the starting point of the year.

For thousands of years, the Celts celebrated the cycle of the seasons as a sign that the universe was in balance. In their world view, everything that lives must die to live again. So, for them, life and death held equally vital places in a repeated pattern, expressed by the seasons of the year. They saw the seasons as a reflection of eternity, endlessly turning from darkness to light and back again.

In this circular image of eternity each thing follows the next in its allotted sequence, like the notes of a tune or the steps in a dance. And because each thing has a vital place in the completed whole, all are equally important.

The Celtic seasons are called **Samhain**, **Imbolc**, **Bealtaine** and **Lughnasa**. On Ireland's Dingle peninsula they still shape the cycle of the year.

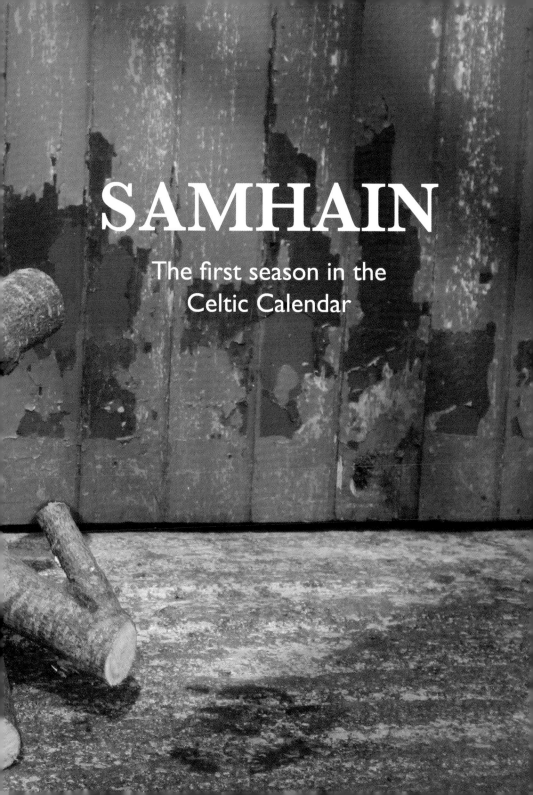

SAMHAIN

The first season in the
Celtic Calendar

NOVEMBER

The First Month of Samhain (Sah-win)

The ancient Celts saw darkness as a fertile state, full of dreams and possibilities. They also believed that turning points between one thing and another offer opportunities for heightened awareness and understanding. So, because November begins the darkest season of the year, the turning point between October and November is one of the most significant dates in their calendar. It begins the season of Samhain which begins the Celtic year.

For the Celts, each day began at sunset, not sunrise, and each new month started at sunset on the last day of the month that had gone before. The start of the season of Samhain was celebrated on 31 October, the night now known in English as Halloween, the Night of the Spirits.

It was believed that at Halloween the dead returned to the homes they'd once lived in on earth. Beloved ancestors were welcomed with fires and feasting, evil spirits were scared off by grotesquely masked dancers, and attempts were made to peer through the veil of time and see the future.

I'm writing this in a stone house in the foothills of the last mountain on Ireland's Dingle peninsula. Living here in a community that balances 21st-century life with a powerful sense of its ancient cultural inheritance, you can still see and feel the links between the changing seasons and the dynamic world view which shaped the rhythms and rituals of the Celtic calendar.

There's nothing escapist or old-fashioned about life here at the western end of the peninsula, but my neighbours' deep respect for their inherited traditions means that many customs and pleasures still flourish here that might otherwise have been lost. My own seasons are shaped by the joys of capturing an awareness of that inheritance in images and words.

For hundreds of years, Irish people have gathered in each others' houses to talk and make music. Along the Atlantic seaboard where Irish (Gaelic), not English, is the first language of the people, this custom, called *bothántaíocht* (buh-hawn-tee-okt), is still recognised as part of the traditional way of life.

Bothántaíocht was once a practical way to economise on light and heat by gathering in one house in a village, where everyone brought a sod of turf for the fire or contributed to the entertainment.

By providing a forum for sharing Ireland's stories, tunes, skills and traditions it has been a vital element in their survival. And a knock at the door here is still a signal to put the kettle on and stir the fire.

My husband Wilf and I take different kinds of photos. I'll point and click when something catches my eye and crop later. He balances light and form while framing the shot. We both try to balance the habit of taking photos with the desire to live, rather than capture, each moment in life as it comes.

Barm Brack

Ingredients

500 g bread flour

¼ level tsp each ground cinnamon
  and nutmeg

½ level tsp salt (optional)

60 g butter (softened)

85 g sugar

25 g yeast

300 ml warm milk

1 egg

250 g sultanas

115 g currants

60 g chopped candied peel

A gold ring

Method

1. Sieve flour, spices and salt into a large mixing bowl and rub in the butter. Stir in the sugar, reserving a teaspoonful. Then cream the yeast, a tsp of sugar and milk and, when the mix froths up, beat the egg into it.

2. Pour the wet mix into the dry one, beating well with a wooden spoon to make the dough. Fold in the dried fruit and peel. Turn out onto a floured surface and knead briefly.

3. Place the dough in a clean bowl and cover with a cloth. Leave in a warm place for 1–3 hours till it has risen to twice its size. Then turn it out and knead briefly to form a cake, incorporating the ring (wrapped in a scrap of greaseproof paper if you like.)

4. Cover the dough and leave it to rise again for about 30 mins. Then bake the cake on a greased baking sheet at 200 °C for about an hour. Test with a skewer before taking out of the oven.

5. Cool on a wire tray and serve in slices with butter.

Also called Barn Brack, it toasts very well and is delicious with jam or strong cheddar cheese.

Modern Halloween traditions echo ancient Samhain rituals. The slice containing the ring foretells a marriage.

Samhain fires invoked
protection and
prefigured the warmth
of spring.

By now harvests are saved and cattle brought down from high fields. Fishermen's craft are secured against storms. Fuel for stoves and fires is gathered or ordered. Children are more likely to be glued to PlayStations than listening to stories, but the traditional skills of the storyteller are valued and passed on; and music making is still a central part of life. Neighbours who text to arrange music sessions will turn up with wine, or an apple tart, in the same way that their grandparents arrived with a sod of turf for the fire. Here on the Dingle peninsula *bothántaíocht* has never really gone away.

Many of Ireland's jigs, reels, polkas, slides and hornpipes came from England and Scotland in the eighteenth and nineteenth centuries, and were incorporated into local tradition.

The *Sean-nós* (shan-noas) songs and airs often heard here on winter evenings belong to a tradition that's older still. The term 'sean-nós' simply means 'the old way'.

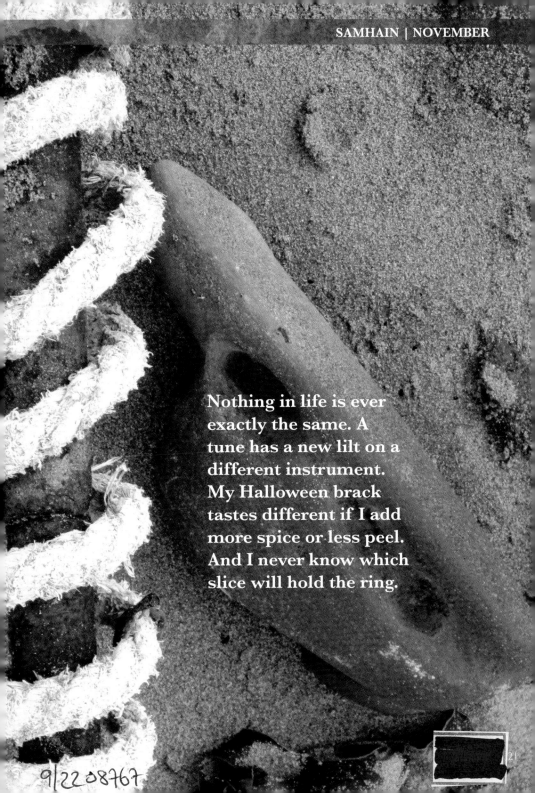

Nothing in life is ever
exactly the same. A
tune has a new lilt on a
different instrument.
My Halloween brack
tastes different if I add
more spice or less peel.
And I never know which
slice will hold the ring.

9/22 08767

DECEMBER

The Second Month of Samhain

December is all about preparation, anticipation and fulfilment, and the specific times at which things must happen are part of the pleasure of the process. When I was a child Christmas began when my mother brought out the 'good' china and glasses that only appeared once a year. My own favourite job was cleaning the silver. There was a silver-plated coffee pot, a wedding present to my mother from the girls in the shop that she'd worked in before she was married, a silver sugar sifter and thin, shining teaspoons.

I still start Christmas each year by polishing the silver. I love the gleaming curves and lines revealed by the rhythmic circling of the cloth. Each year as I go through that ritual taught to me by my mother, I've seen my hands getting more and more like hers as I remember them. Though she never saw my kitchen in Corca Dhuibhne, her spoons and her coffee pot, the china she treasured and the glasses she inherited from her own mother are part of my Christmas today.

In my childhood the pleasure of polishing the silver prefigured the excitement of unpacking the Christmas tree ornaments that lived in a cardboard box in the attic and were lifted down each year by my father.

The ancient Celts' midwinter festival took place at the time of the winter solstice, which occurs in the northern hemisphere around 21 December. It's the annual turning point that reverses the process of the gradual lengthening of the nights and shortening of the days that brings the darkness of winter. At this time of scarcity and cold, they feasted in optimistic celebration of the fruitful months to come.

For the pagan Celts, midwinter was the time when their fertility goddess was pregnant with the longer, lighter days of spring. In the Christian tradition Mary's child, born in December, is known as The Light of the World. Each world view echoes the other, imagining and expressing the same hopes and fears.

Within living memory every door here was left unlocked on Christmas Eve, and the candles that are still placed in the windows are symbolic offerings of welcome and warmth, gifts to the Holy Family on their way to Bethlehem.

Chocolate Truffles

Ingredients

300 g dark chocolate (at least 70% cocoa solids)
300 ml double cream
I knob unsalted butter
A pinch of salt and a splash of brandy (optional)
Chopped nuts/desiccated coconut/cocoa powder

Method

1. Break chocolate into small pieces and put them into a saucepan.

2. In another pan heat cream gently till just bubbling and add the butter.

3. When the butter has melted, pour the mixture over the chocolate pieces and, whisking as you go, melt them slowly over a gentle heat. (Add a spoonful of boiling water if the mixture splits)

4. When it has all come together smoothly, add the pinch of salt and the splash of brandy. Pour into a bowl and leave to set for two hours in the fridge. Bring back to room temperature – about 30 mins.

5. Then, working quickly, make balls of the mixture using two teaspoons and dipping the spoons in boiling water between each spoonful. Swirl the truffles quickly, a few at a time, in a wide, shallow bowl of cocoa powder to coat them evenly and keep them round.

For variety, roll some in chopped nuts or desiccated coconut.

They keep for about a week in a tin or in the fridge.

Home-made sweets and chocolates are great Christmas gifts.

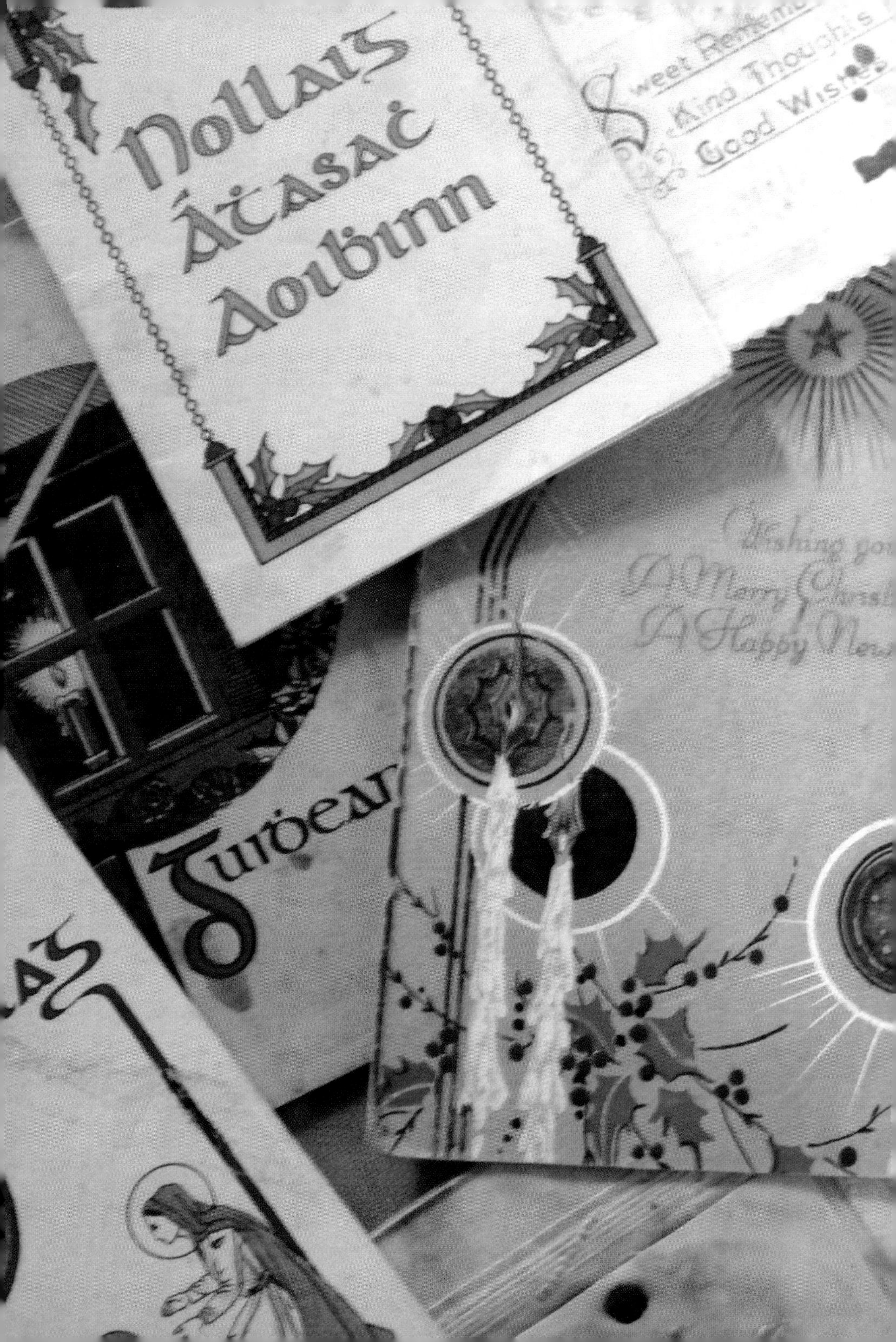
Nollaiġ
Áṫasaċ
Aoiḃinn

I love the idea of midwinter feasting, but enough is plenty. So, although the full Christmas lunch of turkey, ham and all the trimmings is common now all over Ireland, we often have bits and pieces through the day instead. When we do, our main meal might be a smoked salmon salad or maybe a winter soup, rich with root vegetables and flavoured with hints of warming ginger and festive oranges.

Then, between present-giving, mountain walks in the crisp air, and visits to the neighbours, there are sandwiches casually assembled in the kitchen and home-made cakes or locally made cheeses eaten by the fire with a pot of strong tea or a glass of mulled wine.

Each year we drive to Dingle town to buy the sugar, flour, nuts, spices, lemons and dried fruit that combine to fill the house with all the familiar smells of festive cooking and baking.

Wilf and I have a Christmas tree but it isn't a spruce or a fir. Instead, decorated, and anchored by stones in a galvanised bucket, a naked branch cut from an alder or a willow tree sparkles in the firelight. Outside, beyond the flickering candles in the windows, starlight on holly berries in the garden mirrors the blooming branch indoors.

Whenever and wherever human beings bring light to darkness by feasting in winter, the same images appear. The pagan Celts decorated their homes with evergreens to symbolise and promote the return of growth in spring; but until fairly recently, the modern custom of setting up a Christmas tree was largely an urban one in Ireland. Rural homes were usually decorated with holly and ivy and paper 'mottos' wishing blessings on the household.

Here in Corca Dhuibhne ancient and modern rituals coexist and complement each other, bringing deeper, archaic layers of meaning to the darkest month of the year. 26 December, known as The Wran's Day, offers a perfect example. An echo of ancient winter fertility rites, it continues to be celebrated here with rhythms and rituals from a dream state beyond words.

JANUARY

The Third Month of Samhain

New Year in the new calendar – as opposed to the Celtic one – is celebrated with parties and fireworks here, as elsewhere. The traditional twelve days of Christmas end on 6 January when, according to the Christian story, three wise kings were led by a star to the stable where Jesus was born. In Ireland, their feast is known as *Oíche na dTrí Ríthe* (Ee-huh na Dree Ree-huh), which means 'the night of the three kings'. On that night, the last of the Christmas season, three candles shine in the windows here in their honour.

But 6 January has another name as well. It's *Nollaig na mBan* (Null-ig na Mon), which means 'women's Christmas'. Traditionally, it's a night when men take over the household work and women of all generations gather together to eat, dance, sing and enjoy each other's company.

Hospitality and generosity have always been valued here, and the deliberate placing of lights in uncurtained windows during the twelve days of Christmas signals the welcome to be found within. These days, women tend to dress up and go out to restaurants together for *Nollaig na mBan*, but in the past they celebrated in each others' homes, making the last night of the festive season a time for community as well as family.

Then, with all the excitement over, the last month of Samhain offers a tranquil space in which to revisit the past and dream of the future.

I love the calm that returns to the house after Christmas. The grey and creamy-white undecorated walls, the uncluttered surfaces and unhurried days, and the quiet times when precious memories and favourite books can be rediscovered.

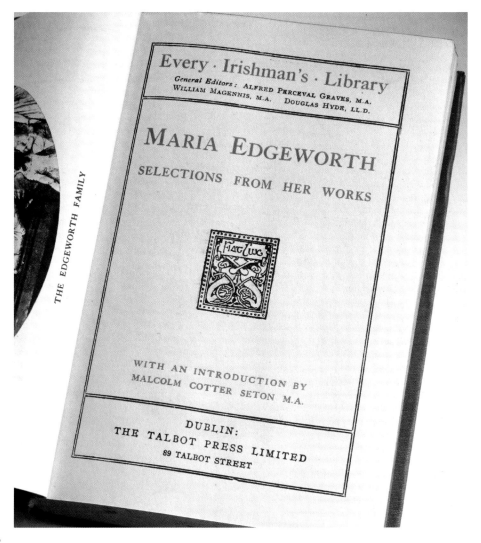

THE EDGEWORTH FAMILY

Every · Irishman's · Library

General Editors: ALFRED PERCEVAL GRAVES, M.A.
WILLIAM MAGENNIS, M.A.   DOUGLAS HYDE, LL.D.

MARIA EDGEWORTH

SELECTIONS FROM HER WORKS

WITH AN INTRODUCTION BY
MALCOLM COTTER SETON M.A.

DUBLIN:
THE TALBOT PRESS LIMITED
89 TALBOT STREET

This is the time to turn over old linen, to make and mend, and to remember and pass on the stories that belong to treasured family heirlooms. Looking at the fine lace made by my great-aunt, I remember the faint scent of lavender in my granny's house in Enniscorthy. Lifting a tray cloth cross-stitched by my mother, I hear the click of the needle against her thimble as she drew blue, brown and dull red threads through the fabric or feather-stitched the hem.

Imperceptibly, the days get longer. But despite the optimism of their midwinter feasting, our ancestors must have lived with fear as well as hope as they waited for spring. Uncertainty bred superstition. This was a month when girls enacted time-honoured rituals to provoke dreams of their future husbands, and when housewives knocked specially baked cakes of bread three times against the door frame before throwing them into the night as a charm against hunger.

On January walks with Wilf, the bones of the land seem exposed to our cameras. Field patterns stripe the mountains like giants' tablecloths laid out to dry. One day, the ocean lies flat as a blue plate. Next day, familiar sandy beaches become cauldrons of heaving stones.

Nourished by seaweed drawn from the beach, and swelled by summer rain, carrots and parsnips emerge from the shed as sound as on the day they were harvested. Onions and herbs stored in the kitchen add flavour to winter stews in which meat and stock just give background depth to the sweet, rich winter vegetables.

Winter Stew

In a heavy pan over a medium
heat, soften a chopped onion
or two in good oil. Clean, peel
and chop whatever root veg you
have to hand. Dice some mutton,
toss in flour with chopped dried
herbs, and seal it in the oniony
oil. Add the veg, plus a handful of
barley or lentils, stirring to allow
the flavours to mingle and adding
a little meat or vegetable stock
if it sticks. Then fill the pan with
stock, cover, boil, and simmer for
at least two and a half hours.

The first woman to live in this house was called Neillí or, in English, Nellie. Her father's name was Muiris, or Maurice, so the neighbours knew her as 'Maurice's Nellie', which in Irish is Neillí Mhuiris (Nelly Wirrish). Neillí and her mother came to live here about 1915, when the thatched cabins at the end of the village were condemned and stone, slate-roofed dwellings were built to rehouse the inhabitants.

My neighbours remember her as a laughing, powerful woman, warm, welcoming and fond of children. After her mother died, she married a man called Paddy Martin. They had no children of their own, but this became a great house for *bothántaíocht*. Neillí's brother James is remembered too, as a quiet man who loved playing cards in the evenings but always left his winnings on the table. They say he had no interest in money; what he valued was the game and good company.

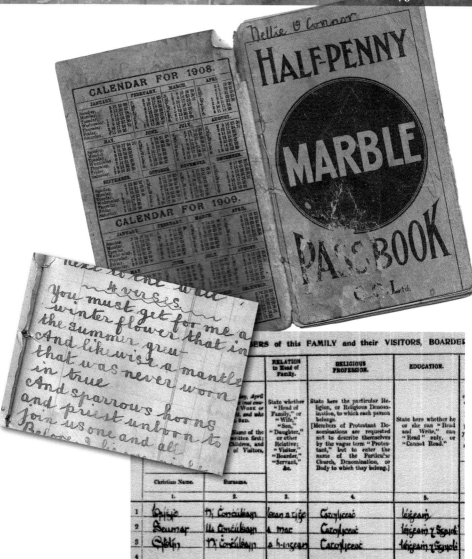

After Neillí and Paddy died, our neighbour Jack Flaherty found papers in her handwriting thrown out on a ditch in the rain. He rescued a little notebook in which, over the years, she had copied out songs and poems in English. Her handwriting can also be seen on the census form of 1911: but she filled that out in Irish, a brave gesture to make at a time of political upheaval in Ireland.

In Ireland, the word 'foosthering,' which comes from the Irish verb *fústar*, means 'rummaging around' or 'wasting time'. To me, time spent foosthering is never wasted.

I treasure my neighbours' memories of Neillí's life in this house as I treasure my memories of my mother, my grandmothers and all the women whose stories enrich and inform my own. The objects they used and loved can still bring them vividly to life.

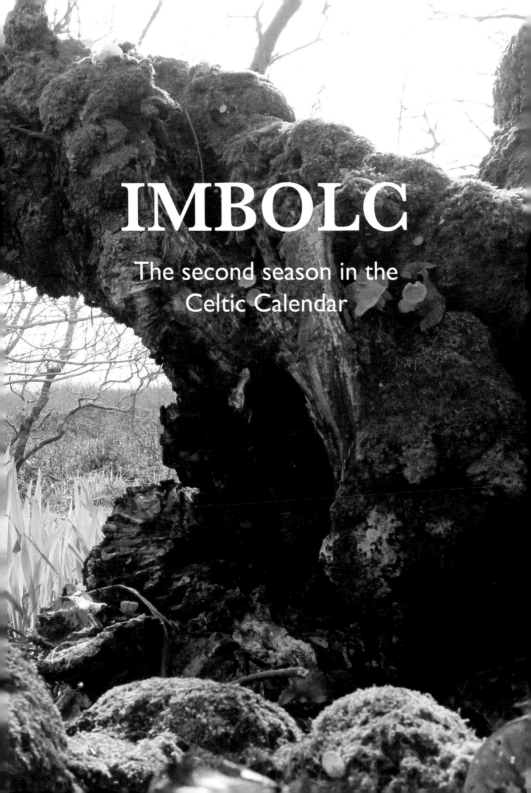

IMBOLC

The second season in the
Celtic Calendar

FEBRUARY

The First Month of Imbolc (Im-bulk)

The word Imbolc comes from the Irish *i mbolg* which means 'in the belly.' At this time of year, the ancient Celts enacted rituals to promote pregnancy in their flocks.

Although stored food would have been running out and weeks would pass before fresh food became available, February was identified as the turning point between winter and spring.

Living close to nature, our ancestors perceived subtle changes in their environment with remarkable levels of intensity. By walking in the countryside and working in the garden, by focusing on small things and cropping images on my computer, I'm learning to recapture a sense of that awareness.

February brings both the promise of change and the need for patience.

For centuries farmers here have used seaweed to fertilise their land. In January and February easterly and northerly winds bring violent gales to the peninsula, ripping weed from the ocean bed and hurling it onto the beaches. Then, in unpredictable sunny breaks in the stormy weather, the seaweed is forked into trailers, or stuffed by hand into bags, and drawn home behind rattling tractors. Rich in minerals, it dries and rots down when spread on the earth, suppressing unwanted couch grass and weeds and fertilising fields and gardens before the spring planting.

The ocean offers
the means to
nourish the land.

St Brigid's Day, 1 February, marks the first day of spring in the Irish Christian tradition. Brigid has always been as highly revered here as St Patrick. Like the goddess Danú, she brings healing and fertility through water, without which there can be no life.

Danú's name means 'water' and echoes of her worship are found in rituals and legends later linked to Brigid. On St Brigid's Eve, ribbons and scraps of fabric were left out on bushes to catch the dew and then carefully kept for use when tending the sick.

Both Brigid and Danú were said to wake the earth in springtime by the touch of their feet on the land. Each was a powerful, matriarchal figure associated with fire and light. Myths and legends also associate them with bees, and with the antiseptic, antibacterial properties of honey.

St Brigid's crosses, woven out of rushes on her feast day, are still made and hung over doorways to protect households and farm animals throughout the year. The earliest versions, which had three arms, not four, are said to have been representations of the rays of the sun.

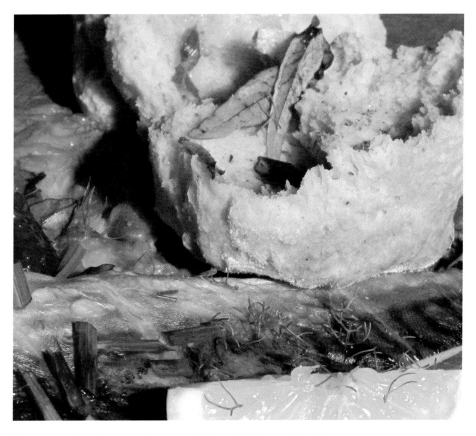

Salted mackerel was a winter staple here in Corca Dhuibhne.
I love it smoked and served with home-made chutney,
peppery scones, and a garnish of overwintered chard and
the year's first garlic leaves.

For the scones, rub 85 g of butter into 225 g of self-raising flour with a pinch of salt and a grind of black pepper. Work 3 tbsp of buttermilk and a beaten egg lightly into the mix with your hand to make a soft dough. You can add a scatter of flour if the mix is too wet. Pat into a round about 3 cm thick. Cut scones. Bake on a floured sheet for around 10 minutes at 200 °C.

The trick is to make these as quickly as you can and to pat, not roll out, the dough when you cut them.

Decisions made in February dictate what and how Wilf and I will eat in the coming months. We save much of our own seed from year to year and swop surplus stocks with the neighbours. In Dingle town, as the weeks go by, onion sets and seed potatoes begin to appear in shop windows.

Hens don't naturally lay eggs in winter because they need about fifteen hours of light each day to keep their reproductive system active. So, for those kept in natural conditions, the laying season begins towards the end of this first month of Imbolc.

Last year, I became fascinated by the slow processes that produce the spirits made in Dingle town's distillery. It takes time, darkness and the mild, moist air of the peninsula to allow the two casks of whiskey made there each day to mature. 'Making whiskey', I was told, 'is all about patience.'

So is gardening. It takes time, the darkness of the earth, the light and heat of the sun, and the life-giving force of the rain to release the glossy green leaves within these spinach seeds.

MARCH

The Second Month of Imbolc

An Irish expression often used in springtime is *bíonn fad coiscéim coiligh ar an lá* (been fod kush-came quillig air on law). It means 'there's a stretch in the day that's the length of a cockerel's footstep'.

March is the month of the spring equinox when, after weeks of barely perceptible change, day and night finally move into perfect balance. To the ancient Celts it was a time for purification and for ritual celebrations to promote lactation in goats and ewes. Now, in the twenty-first century, the hills here around the house are still loud with the cries of sheep and lambs.

On 17 March in Ireland, the traditional weeks of fasting before Easter are interrupted by parties and parades in honour of St Patrick. It seems likely that the Christian Church's choice of date for the saint's day, and the legend of how he disrupted a druidic ritual on the Hill of Tara, contain folk memories of new Christian rites replacing older, pagan responses to the equinox.

In the past almost every family here kept cows. Surplus milk was sold to the local creamery and butter was often taken on horseback over the mountains to market in Cork.

Many farmers and fishermen here still like to chew Dillisk. It's a pungent, salty, red seaweed now used to flavour one of Dingle's best-known artisan cheeses.

Cattle were once a measure of wealth in Irish society. In early medieval stories and poems, descriptions of warriors feasting on dairy produce are metaphors for the power and generosity of Ireland's chieftains and kings.

The old people in Ireland said soup made from the first greens of the season was great for cleansing the blood. Herbs and vegetables from the garden were supplemented by young nettle and dandelion leaves.

In the past, people's nutrient reserves were running low by this time of year and their bodies craved fresh vegetables. Bursting with antioxidants and folic acid, spring greens support healthy organ and immune function.

Like the custom of spring-cleaning our homes, the idea that eating new greens was cleansing may be an echo of ancient purification rites once held at the spring equinox.

Grow them free from pesticides or artificial fertilisers, bring them straight from the garden to the kitchen, and wilt them in garlic-infused oil or butter in a heavy-based pan. Then simmer gently in spring water for 5 or 10 minutes, and pass your soup through a fine sieve or blitz it smooth with a stick blender.

The weather here in March is always uncertain. Some years,
as I dodge through the fields between sunshine and showers,
it's hard to find the shamrock traditionally worn in Ireland
on St Patrick's Day. But even in a rough year when growth is
slow, farmers like our neighbour Jack always know where to
look for it.

St Patrick's associations with the shamrock and the colour green may, in fact, be comparatively modern. Legend says that he used the three-leaved shamrock to explain the concept of the Holy Trinity but, as the pagan Celts were familiar with triple-aspect deities, that story is likely to have been invented in the Middle Ages.

It was recorded that 'the poorer people' in Ireland wore shamrock on St Patrick's Day in 1681 but a reference from 1628 describes Irish soldiers as wearing crosses of red ribbon 'after their country manner'.

There's no doubt that the shamrock is St Patrick's symbol these days, though, and all over the world on 17 March people wear green in his honour.

Local parades take place in small towns and villages all over Ireland, with representation from shops and businesses, schools, and musicians and dancers on lorries, and on trailers pulled by tractors. The most westerly St Patrick's Day celebrations in Corca Dhuibhne are held in the village of Ballyferriter.

Now that St Patrick's Day has gone global, huge festivities take place in capital cities from Tokyo to New York. World-famous landmarks like Niagara Falls and the Sydney Opera House are floodlit in green, and the legend of the escaped slave boy who returned to convert his captors has been turned into a branding exercise which promotes Ireland's tourist industry.

But there's nothing new about that. The legend of St Patrick has always been about promotion and brand image. It's a mixture of folklore, medieval church propaganda, and political acquisition, which has grown and changed across more than a thousand years according to how different groups and generations have wanted to see and make use of it.

As far as we know, though, a historical Patrick did exist. There are two fifth-century manuscripts attributed to him, neither of which has any reference to shamrocks, driving snakes out of Ireland or confounding pagan druids.

According to himself, he was 'a simple country person, a refugee, and unlearned', who, while he believed himself to be inspired by a god, didn't see himself as a saint.

APRIL

The Third Month of Imbolc

People here say that in the past they always set, or planted, potatoes by St Patrick's Day. They also say they can clearly see changes in annual weather patterns which have happened in the course of their lifetime. And if you mention scientific findings on climate change they shake their heads and wonder why no one started by asking farmers or fishermen. But though winters are growing wetter, causing gardeners and farmers to plant later, weather conditions at this time of year have always been uncertain.

There's a folktale about a brindled cow on a mountaintop who boasts that the weather in March can't kill her. So March borrows three days from April and batters the old cow to death with a violent hailstorm. That's why the first three days of April are known in Ireland as *laethanta na riabhaiche* (lay-han-tah nah ree-vock-ah), which means 'the borrowed days'.

Traditional spades were made so that the treadle or step, called *an cúilín* (on cool-een) in Irish, could be fitted either for the right foot or the left.

My earliest memories are of my Galway granny, a capricious, faintly malicious woman, who spent her last years bedridden in our family house in Dublin. What I remember most about her is her silver hair and the sound of her voice telling stories. Looking back now, I know that many of those stories were myths and folktales with roots that reach back across millennia.

I grew interested in folklore as I grew up. One of Ireland's most distinguished folklore scholars, Kevin Danaher, was a family friend. I was fascinated by his descriptions of old customs and traditions, and by the turns of phrase that migrated from Irish to English as the native language declined.

From the late nineteenth century onwards, English became the spoken norm in most of Ireland. But the western end of the Dingle Peninsula is what's known as a *Gaeltacht* (gwale-tokt) area, where Irish continues to be the language of everyday life and the medium through which children are educated. That's part of the reason why Ireland's oral cultural inheritance is preserved and passed on here so effectively.

There are Old, Middle and Modern forms of Irish, just as in English, and a standardised form of modern spelling and grammar was introduced in 1958.

Everyone in contemporary Ireland learns Irish in school. But like Neillí, the first woman who lived in this house, who penned her songbook in English and completed her census form in Irish, children in Gaeltacht areas today live bilingual lives. There are three distinct dialects spoken along the Atlantic seaboard: Ulster, Connacht and Munster Irish. Because standardisation happened relatively recently and the Irish language culture is essentially an oral one, local pronunciation, spelling and grammar survive and thrive.

The old flowing Irish script used by Neillí is no longer taught in schools. Today printed Irish uses Roman typefaces, though the Irish alphabet doesn't include the letters j, k, q, v, w, x, y or z. Accented vowels indicate a lengthened sound in speech – the 'í' at the end of Neillí's name, for example, which is pronounced 'ee'.

The history of the Irish language has been shaped by the evolving politics and policies of almost eight centuries of British rule. As in many colonised countries, the first English settlers considered the indigenous language barbaric. Later, though many of its scholars came from the largely Protestant Anglo-Irish gentry, Irish came to be associated with Catholicism, sedition, and the 'uneducated' rural poor.

In the eighteenth century, in an attempt to force all British subjects to conform to Anglicanism, Catholic schools were outlawed. As a result, many wealthy Irish families educated their children in France, Italy or Spain, while 'hedge schools' at home continued to teach the rural poor. Theoretically illegal, and sometimes literally held under hedgerows, these schools continued an ancient, mainly oral, process of education through Irish. Some taught Greek and Latin. In 1756, a few miles from the village where I'm writing this, there was 'a Latin school, chiefly supported by a small stipend of three pounds a year' bequeathed by an Irish canon lawyer educated in Paris.

In 1831, the British government set up a national school system in Ireland with the aim of 'uniting in one system children of different creeds'. It also aimed to ensure that they spoke English. Children had 'tally sticks' hung round their necks and were beaten according to the number of the notches that were added to the stick each time they were heard speaking Irish. Parents often assisted in the process, fearful that Irish would hinder their children's prospects if they emigrated to America. That fear persisted within living memory, while other families resolutely preserved the language as a precious inheritance.

As Neillí was growing up, Irish, which everyone in this area would have learned from the cradle, had begun to be taught in schools, and by nationalist and cultural revival groups. When an independent state was established, Irish was confirmed as its official language and in 2007 it became an official working language of the European Union.

Wherever an indigenous language is threatened, high on the list of potential losses to future generations is the sense of cultural identity that is preserved in local folklore. In 1937 the Irish Folklore Commission initiated a revolutionary collection scheme: schoolchildren were given books in which to write down their parents' and grandparents' folktales, riddles and proverbs, songs, customs and beliefs, games, pastimes, traditional crafts and work practices. It resulted in more than half a million manuscript pages of material. And here at the westernmost end of the Dingle peninsula, as in other Gaeltacht areas, those memories were all preserved in Irish.

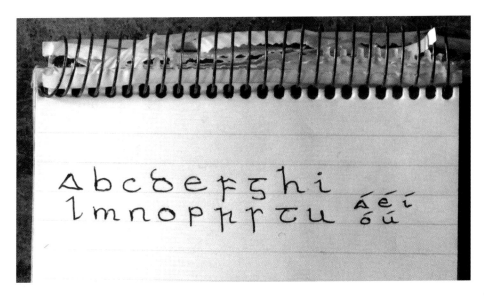

Jack Flaherty says that when he was a child no one had chocolate eggs at Easter time. Round here, they used to boil a big pot of hens' or ducks' eggs on Easter Sunday morning and compete to see who could eat the most of them.

In an Easter custom that is almost forgotten now, well-off Irish farmers once sent presents of portions of beef to their poorer neighbours. Often the animal had been slaughtered early in winter, and the meat salted down. Nowadays in Ireland it's usual to eat lamb with new greens at Easter time. But the memory of 'corned beef and cabbage' as a festive meal crossed the Atlantic with the emigrants and still survives in America.

In Irish folklore, witches disguised as hares have power over livestock and land.

Easter Cake

Ingredients

110 g each self-raising flour, caster
  sugar and butter at room temperature
1 tsp baking powder
2 large eggs
2–3 drops vanilla essence
Good chocolate for decoration, lemon curd and cream

Method

1. Holding sieve high, sieve flour and baking powder into a large bowl. Add other ingredients and whisk.

2. Divide batter between 2 x 18 cm sponge tins, 3.5 cm deep, lined with baking parchment or greased paper.

3. Bake for 30 mins on top shelf at 170 °C.

4. Remove from tins immediately and cool on a wire tray. Sandwich with lemon curd and decorate with chocolate curls and/or (organically grown) flowers.

Double the quantities and go for four layers if you fancy being a champion Easter egg-eater.

My favourite recipe for an Easter cake is
simplicity itself. A two-egg sponge layered
with cream and lemon curd, decorated
with curls of chocolate.

BEALTAINE

The Third season in the
Celtic Calendar

MAY

The First Month of Bealtaine (Bee-owl-tin-neh)

May Day, on 1 May, is celebrated throughout the northern hemisphere as the first day of summer. Here in Ireland the roots of the festival lie in ancient Celtic rituals held at the turning point between the seasons of Imbolc and Bealtaine. The word Bealtine, said to come from *Bel Tine* which means 'Bel Fire', is the Irish language word for the month of May. Bel was one of the names of the Celtic sun god whose power was symbolised by fire. Ritual re-enactments of his marriage to the fertility goddess were believed to promote the sunshine and rainfall required for crops to thrive.

Here in Corca Dhuibhne May brings a new awareness of the garden. Each day, from first light, the air rings with birdsong. Nesting crows creak past overhead. Bees hum on blossoms and tiny, blood-red fuchsia buds shine against deep green foliage. One year behind the old byre I found flowers on a pear tree which, two years previously, we'd liberated from a supermarket. It had been a sad, dry stick with its roots wrapped in plastic. Now each year, as the sap rises, it promises baked fruit puddings flavoured with ginger and honey.

In Ireland, as imagery merged across millennia, the blossom which once symbolised Danú's fertility became a symbol, on May altars, of the Virgin Mary's purity.

All human beings have an instinct for ritual. For me summer begins when I can sit out in the garden with my coffee.

Easy
Shortbread
Biscuits

Beat 100 g of butter with a wooden spoon until soft. Beat in 50 g of caster sugar followed by 125 g plain flour. Bring the mix together and knead it to a smooth ball. Transfer to a lightly sugared board and roll out to about ½ cm thick. Cut biscuits and bake on a greased baking sheet at 160 °C for 10–20 mins.

They're done when they are a golden biscuity brown. A scatter of brown sugar as soon as they come out of the oven will add crunch. Then let them cool on a wire rack.

This year we emerged from a music session in the second week in May to find snow on our car. Only a few hours earlier the evening had been balmy. That's not unusual during the weeks between mid April and mid May known here in Ireland as *Scairbhín na gCuach* (Skar-a-veen nah Goo-ok), 'the rough month of the cuckoo'.

Scairbhín na gCuach brings sudden dips in temperature, unexpected changes in wind direction and violent showers of hailstones, sleet and snow. It also brings cloudless blue skies, jade green and indigo lights on the ocean, and days of glorious sunshine.

I don't know why this month belongs to the cuckoo. Maybe it's because her song heralds less changeable weather to come.

The sharpness of the Scairbhín's contrasts makes it a time of heightened awareness.

Watching the sky, we can tell which beach we should walk on. If there's rain on the wind from the north, we choose the long, curving strand below the village which, in English, is called Ventry. If clouds blow in from the west, we'll drive to the beach called *Béal Bán* (Bee-al Bawn), which means 'The White Mouth'. Cattle graze in fields that border its white sand and across the bay you can see the high bulk of Mount Brandon, which dominates the peninsula.

In the past, cosmetics as well as healing remedies were often prepared at home. There's a wonderful book called *A Natural History of Ireland*, written in 1652, which describes 'gentlewomen in Ireland' gathering 'a good store of dew' in Maytime. They used it to wash their faces to prevent freckles, sunburn and wrinkles during the coming year. Kept in bottles and applied to the eyes, it was also said to ensure clear eyes in the morning after even the shortest sleep.

In his book *The Year In Ireland*, Kevin Danaher says that dew or water taken from a neighbour's farm between sunset on May Eve and sunrise on May Day was thought to have great powers for good or evil. Sometimes young girls raced each other or sat up all night to be first to get it.

All sorts of charms for telling fortunes were used as well. Here's one from Lady Wilde's *Ancient Cures, Charms and Usages*, published in 1890.

On a May morning, before sunrise, go out to the garden, and the first snail you see take up, and put it on a plate sprinkled lightly with flour, place a cabbage-leaf over, and so leave it till after sunrise, when you will find the initial letters of your lover's name traced on the flour.

If the snail was in his shell when you found him, your lover would be rich, but if he was 'out of his house' your future husband would be poor and have no home to take you to.

In the twenty-first century, as living becomes more complicated and stressful, the urge to control our lives is growing. I suppose that, just as women have always tried to prevent wrinkles, people have always longed to foresee the future. But the truth is that no one can ever tell what will happen next. No matter how much we try to provide for what may lie ahead, the future will always be uncertain.

It's not easy to learn to live in the moment without fear for the future or regrets for the past. But each small pleasure we perceive and enjoy focuses the mind, senses and emotions on what is really happening, instead of on what we hope or fear may happen next.

The detail in birdsong, the texture and taste of food, or the colours and patterns of shells or seeds are all entry points to a richer awareness of the dynamic complexity of which we're just a part.

The Celts' fertility goddess had three aspects, encompassing potential, fulfilment and death. She was the Maiden, the Mother and the Crone, an image of an optimistic world view which saw ageing as a vital stage in a cycle in which death leads to rebirth as inevitably as winter leads to spring.

In rural Ireland, within living memory, it was a May custom for girls to carry a doll, or *bábóg* (baw-bogue), decked in lace and flowers from door to door, singing to welcome the summer. It's a ritual as ancient as the worship of Danú, whom the *bábóg* originally represented. Schoolchildren here in Corca Dhuibhne sing the same song today.

May-time Dolly, Maiden of Summer,
Up each hill and down each glen,
Girls dressed up in bright-white garments,
We brought the Summer along with us.

Bábóg na Bealtaine,
Maighdean an
tSamhraidh,
Suas gach cnoc
is síos gach gleann,
Cailíní maiseacha
bán-gheala gléasta,
Thugamar féin
an Samhradh linn.

JUNE

The Second Month of Bealtaine

I first came to Corca Dhuibhne when I was seventeen, on a scholarship to improve my Irish. I fell in love with the place, its people and its cultural inheritance, but life and work took me to London, where I met Wilf, an opera director who's also a writer. When we came here on our honeymoon he too fell in love with Corca Dhuibhne and for years we treated it as an escape from the pressures of London living.

Then, about fifteen years ago, we found the house where I'm writing this now, and our lives changed completely. Since then we work and live both here and in an inner-city London flat. One of the greatest differences between the two places is that while the flat is a box carved out of a former factory, the house on the side of the mountain has a garden.

When I came to Corca Dhuibhne as a teenager people here had little time or energy to grow anything but food. Flower gardens then were thought of as extravagant. Besides, the wildflowers here are remarkable. In summer the roads are bordered with scarlet and purple fuchsia, orange and neon-green montbretia, meadowsweet, honeysuckle, ferns and twisting briars. Surrounded by all that wild glory the idea of planting individual pansy seeds can seem ludicrous.

Yet when we bought this house we inherited the remains of a flower garden. When Neillí and Paddy died, the house and the land immediately around it were left to a retired couple called Con and Lís. Con was a formidable gardener and the memory of his work here lives after him. When Wilf and I arrived, we would often meet neighbours who were interested to know which house we'd come to. The moment we identified it, huge smiles would appear on their faces. 'That house has a lovely garden', they'd say, and go on to describe the flowering shrubs and roses and the immaculate, shaven lawns that were once Con's pride and joy.

By our time, though, the lawns had become a waving meadow and the shrubs were overgrown, not because they hadn't been lovingly tended by the people we had bought from, but because Corca Dhuibhne's mild, humid climate causes huge growth spurts in summer.

Like Con, Wilf's a passionate gardener, but his approach is definitely different. He quite enjoys a sense of wilderness; and, like our older neighbours, when he looks at a piece of land, what he sees is a place to grow his dinner.

When we first arrived here our neighbour Jack used to drop by each day as he passed with his cows. He remembers the stories that belong to this house – where Neillí set her ridges of spuds, and how Paddy, who was a great fisherman, had no interest in working the land. He knows the history of Con's flowers and bushes, how some were bought and how others came from the neighbours. He's the best of friends and neighbours and each word of advice he has given us has been more than worth listening to.

Unlike me with my Dublin childhood, Wilf grew up in rural England, in a household which grew its own vegetables and kept hens. So, as soon as he had scythed the grass and we had subdued the overgrown hedges, he consulted Jack about the best site for our first crops. It turned out to be the site of Con's lawn which from a farmer's point of view had been fallow for years and was just waiting to be cultivated.

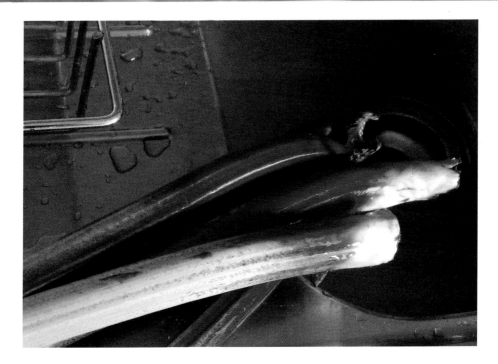

One of the first things Wilf set here was rhubarb. Jack brought it up from his own garden, wrapped in newspaper. Each year in early summer it yields slender pink stalks to be eaten raw, dipped in sugar, or made into a tart sauce for oily fish.

In June, when I pull the bigger, deep red stalks, their shining white ends emerge from the dark earth after a pleasing moment of resistance. Chopped and gently stewed in a few drops of water and honey, they make fillings for June pies and crumbles. And the sweetened juice, strained and diluted with ice-cold water, is the best of thirst-quenching drinks after a long day's gardening.

One of the most significant festivals in the Celtic calendar takes place between 21 and 24 June. It's the period of the summer solstice in the northern hemisphere, also known as midsummer.

As with all turning points, the solstice was seen as a time when the veil between the human and spirit worlds was particularly permeable, and the potential for contact and influence was heightened.

Midsummer Eve is still celebrated here with bonfires. In the past, individual households lit small fires on their land and scattered the ashes at field boundaries to protect their crops and livestock. Then they'd join the neighbours at huge communal fires that were lit at sunset, when people gathered to dance, sing and pray for a good harvest. Boys and men competed to jump through the flames to promote strength, and 'seeds' of fire brought home on shovels were used to light the first fires on the hearths of newly built houses.

Yellow flowers, associated with the sun god, were used in midsummer rituals, and smoke from the communal fires was believed to bring luck and have healing properties.

The Christian feast day of St John falls on 24 June. In Ireland and elsewhere, bonfires in his honour are lit at sunset on St John's Eve. Often they're sited on beaches, hilltops or at boundaries, revealing their connection with ancient midsummer rites.

Medicinal herbs gathered on St John's Day were said to be particularly potent, especially those with yellow flowers. Among their other properties, fennel is an antispasmodic, calendula is anti-inflammatory, and Yellow Mugwort, also known as St John's Herb, is traditionally used for skin complaints.

Using herbs as medicine requires specialist knowledge. Not only are they powerful in themselves but they can interact with prescription drugs, so they shouldn't be used without proper advice.

But herbs and flowers, like vegetables, if grown without pesticides and eaten in moderation, make healthy additions to a balanced diet. I love their colour and flavour in cakes, salads and sandwiches, the slightly bitter freshness of parsley, the way fennel complements fish, and how chives and lemon balm or marjoram in stuffing bring a whole new dimension to roast chicken.

After the rhubarb came up the hill in the cab of Jack's tractor, the gift of comfrey came down from a farm on the mountain above us which belongs to Mike George Mac Gearailt.

Comfrey is a wonderful herb. In Irish, its name is *An Compar* (An Kum-por) which, I think, must just be taken from the English. Because of its traditional use in healing bone fractures, old English country names for it include Knitbone, Knitback and Boneset.

It's also a natural source of nitrogen, phosphorus and potassium for plants. You can add it to the compost heap throughout the summer, or turn the leaves, which decompose quickly because of their low fibre content, into a potent, though smelly, liquid manure.

Put 1 kg of freshly cut comfrey leaves into a 10-litre container. (Don't use metal because rust can add toxic quantities of iron oxide.) Fill with rainwater, and cover with a lid to keep out light. In 2–6 weeks, diluted 1 : 10 with water, it will feed your beans, onions, gooseberries, or anything else you grow that likes potash.

JULY

The Third Month of Bealtaine

In living memory July was known in Ireland as 'the hungry month', when stored grain from the previous year's harvest often ran out. People who kept livestock could live comfortably till the grain in their fields ripened, but families without land or cattle could come close to starvation unless they had help from their neighbours. Traditionally that help was always given and generosity was said to bring good luck.

From about 1750 to the 1840s, market conditions and British government policies changed the balance of Ireland's rural economy. Increased quantities of corn grown for export resulted in increased numbers of landless agricultural labourers. Soon the majority of the rural poor had nothing to eat but potatoes grown on plots let to them by their landlords for labour rent. This lack of balance became catastrophic when blight struck successive potato harvests and the countryside was ravaged by famine, sickness and emigration.

One of the first things our neighbour Jack said when we came here was that nothing in this village goes to waste. That's a philosophy rooted in memories of famine. It is also born of a deep understanding of the fragile sustainability of resources and food sources.

Though my mother wasn't a countrywoman, she had Jack's dislike of waste. She shopped carefully and planned meals so that food seldom went off. In our house we recycled paper bags and string and rubber bands. Used wrapping paper and cardboard were stored behind a window seat, and scrap writing paper in a sideboard. I remember my mother's tin of buttons, some of which had been saved and reused by my Enniscorthy granny before her; when I was small she used to tip them onto a tea tray and tell me to sort them by colour and size. It was the perfect way to keep a child employed for hours.

My mother also had a healthy scepticism about germ-eating, enzyme-filled washing powders and kitchen cleaners. In my teens, watching her cleaning the sink with bicarbonate of soda or polishing windows with newspaper, I thought she was terribly old-fashioned. These days she'd be hailed as an eco-warrior.

Nothing goes to waste here in Neilli's garden. In July, when beans and peas clamber up their cage of trimmed sticks cut from the hedges, pinched-out flowers and pea tops make a garnish for summer lunches of cheese on toast with chives. The delicate flavours hint at the sweet taste of fresh peas to come, and the pinching-out results in healthy offshoots and stronger growth.

Thinned-out beetroot provides salad leaves for sandwiches. The tiny raw beets, chopped very fine, can be scattered on salads.

I looked out the window today and saw that the sun was blazing. One thing I've learnt as a freelance writer is that too much time spent in front of a computer means life can pass you by; so half an hour later I was on my way to a friend's café. It's called *Tigh Áine (Teeg* Awn-yeh), which means 'Áine's House', and that's what it is, a house set low in a steep field above a cliff. Beside it, Áine has built an airy café-restaurant which doubles as an art gallery and, occasionally, a music venue. A broad patio outside has stunning views across the ocean.

Sitting there with my coffee, I watched white-topped waves pounding a distant beach, and listened to the shrill chirp of a gosling that was grazing at my feet. She was hatched from the third of a clutch of three eggs and her mother, deciding that two offspring were enough, refused to rear her. Uncared for, she would have died. Instead she's being painstakingly taught to take her bath and find her own grazing; and when she grows up, her eggs, like those of Áine's ducks and the hens, will be used in the restaurant's baking.

Soon after we came here Wilf decided to take a break from his London work to make time to study traditional Irish music. We'd always known that a musician and a writer in one house needed separate workspaces, so we planned to build a new kitchen. It would be wrapped around a little room for Wilf's desk while I'd continue to work at the other end of the house, where Neillí once cooked on the open fire.

Before foundations for the new room could be dug, we had to demolish a small shed, built of concrete blocks, which had gone up in Con's time against the north gable of the house. Farther up the garden were the remains of a stone byre in which Neillí and Paddy had once kept a donkey. As Wilf and I knocked down the shed, we carried the concrete blocks up to the byre where, with help from Jack's nephew Terry, Wilf used them to extend Paddy's old stone walls to make a sound, new structure, roofed with corrugated iron and faced with old roof slates.

Then from the back of Jack's shed came nine windows, carefully stored since he'd replaced them years before in his own house. Light now filters through them onto our garden tools and a battered old harmonium that was dumped in a car park in the rain.

Nothing goes
to waste in
this village.

Like many indigenous tribespeople today, the ancient Celts seem to have believed that all things were contained within all other things, and that everything in the universe shared a living soul.

That world view makes no distinction between what we call animate and inanimate objects. So in it, tools and stones, animals and humans, plants and metals, all require equal care and respect.

Along with that belief system comes a deep sense of responsibility for the continuing health of the planet. No resource should be drained to a point beyond regeneration, the interaction of ecosystems must be recognised and respected, and nothing should be taken away unless something is given back. Awareness of the consequences of our actions is demanded of us because balance can't be maintained effectively unless everyone's individual behaviour is recognised as part of the equation.

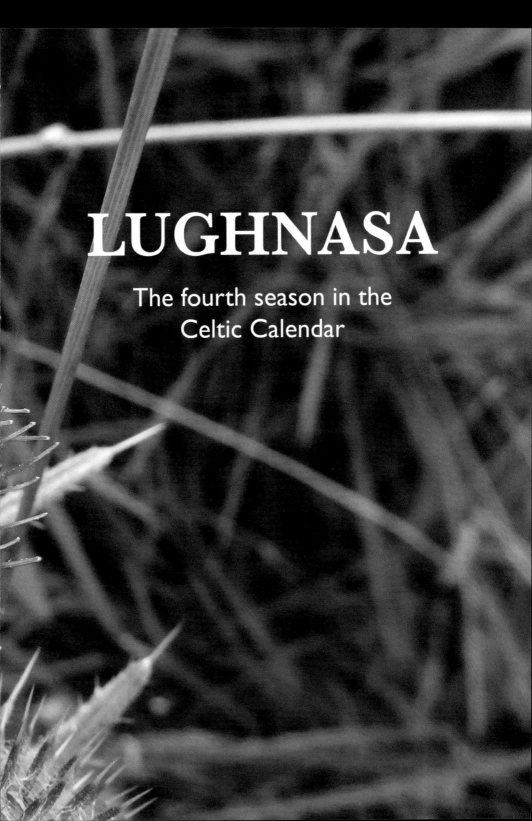

LUGHNASA

The fourth season in the
Celtic Calendar

AUGUST

The First Month of Lughnasa (Loo-nah-sah)

This is the first month of the last season of the Celtic year. Lughnasa, the name of the season, is also the Irish for August. The root of the word is the name of the Celtic god Lugh and for centuries scholars have argued about its meaning. Some say it comes from a word which means 'bright' or 'shining.' Others think it may mean 'black' or that it derives from the verb 'to swear', or make an oath.

Lugh was probably worshipped in different aspects across different Celtic territories which, at various times, reached as far east as the site of the modern city of Ankara and as far west as Ireland's Atlantic seaboard. Here in Corca Dhuibhne where the Earth Mother's name was Danú, Lugh was a derivation of the Celts' supreme deity, and appears, like Bel, to have been a Sky Father, identified with the sun.

He's associated with this time of year because of the importance of fine weather conditions to promote the successful harvesting of crops.

At this time of year, whenever neighbours meet, we exchange updates on the state of our potato crop. Until recently most people here also made hay and harvested grain. To begin when a crop is still unripe or to risk it being spoilt by worsening weather can still affect whole communities and their animals throughout the coming winter.

It has always taken experience and judgment to decide on the optimum moment, and in the past families in each village often worked together to ensure that everyone's crops would be safely gathered in.

Because the process was both vital and uncertain, hopes and fears once expressed in ancient rituals survived within living memory as harvest superstitions. In Irish, a hare fleeing the reapers was often called an *cailleach* (on kal-yok), which means 'the hag' or 'the witch', and it was bad luck to own the last field in which she took refuge. 'Hunting' or 'putting out' the hare was the expression commonly used for completing the harvest.

Our neighbours remember the days of putting out the hare, and the custom of leaving a single sheaf standing in the field at the end of the harvest. In some areas the last sheaf was also known as '*an cailleach*' and carried in procession from the field. The identification of the hare and the sheaf with supernatural female powers are echoes of ceremonial thanksgiving to the Earth Goddess.

All over rural Ireland this is the traditional time of year for fairs and markets, gatherings and horse racing. I love the crowds and conviviality, old friends meeting, bets being placed, deals being done, and the timeless sense of communities coming together.

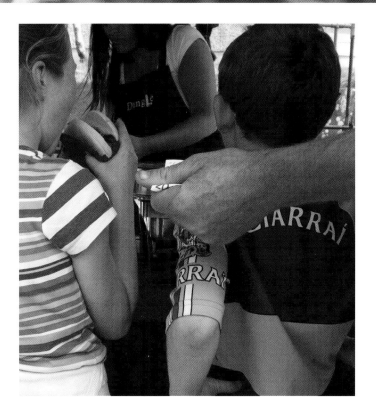

For the ancient Celts seasonal gatherings seem to have incorporated both spiritual and material dimensions and they gave equal importance to each. They were communal occasions at which marriages were made, livestock was traded and rituals were enacted. Often they took place on mountaintops, near freshwater sources, or by the sea.

Beach races at Lughnasa are an ancient tradition, reaching back to harvest rituals that celebrated Lugh's association with horses. Here at the end of the peninsula there are annual races on Béal Bán. People sit on the dunes eating picnics and looking out across the curving, mile-long stretch of white sand at the flat, turquoise ocean and the high, blazing sky. When the horses streak by, foam flying back from their bits and sand from their hooves, the riders' satin jackets and the animals' rippling muscles shine like the sun god's spear of light.

129

While some crops still require patience, there's great pleasure to be had this month from early pickings. Nothing beats the flavour of little carrots or crunchy radishes washed under the garden tap and eaten raw in the open air.

Each year when I pick the first of the peas, I'm torn between eating them straight from the pod or steaming them for the few minutes that help to bring out their sweetness.

Changing calendars and weather conditions, and different crops planted by different communities across centuries, have meant that the harvest season here has variously been reckoned to stretch from the end of July to late September. In many areas the struggle between the sun god Lugh and his enemy *Crom Dubh* (Krum Duv), 'The Crooked Dark One,' is still celebrated on the last Sunday of July. Elsewhere the festival takes place in August. In the earliest stories of all it's the Dark One who rescues a shining goddess from the underworld; in Celtic mythology Lugh defeats Crom and restores the threatened harvest; and in the Christian tradition Crom Dubh was a pagan chieftain defeated by St Brendan or St Patrick.

The release of a shining goddess imprisoned in darkness and the triumph of the sun god over his dark enemy are images of the successful harvest of ripened grain.

The other day I asked Jack if there is a particular word for the end of the harvest. He said that here at the end of the Dingle peninsula it's known in Irish as *an closúr* (on clo-soor). The word comes from the Latin *clausura* which means closure or conclusion, so it must have come into the language with the arrival of Christianity. But the sense of pleasure and relief when crops are safely gathered in is as ancient as the stories of Lugh and Crom Dubh.

SEPTEMBER

The Second Month of Lughnasa

As the year moves towards its next seasonal turning point, the steady rhythm of the seasons provides a familiar background against which awareness of change can become more acute. The days shorten and sunlight slants through the back windows here in the house, complicating the patterns made by flames on the hearthstone. When I walk the roads between fuchsia hedgerows, I reach between glossy green leaves to pull out last year's dry sticks for use as kindling.

September often brings stunning weather to the peninsula. All through the month farmers work late in the fields and farmyards. Here in Neillí's garden Wilf and I pick beans and lift spuds while flights of house martins wheel overhead, preparing to migrate. Behind the house windfall apples disappear almost as soon as they drop from the trees into the long grass. They're eaten by insects and field mice.

Light changes. The colours of flowers intensify in the hedgerows and mist softens the contours of Mount Brandon. Everywhere there's plenty and the need to gather it in.

One September a few years ago Wilf was working in the garden when a stranger stopped at our gate and, after they'd chatted, wandered in to admire our crop of late spuds. Then, having checked out the parsnips and turnips, refused a cup of tea because he was in a hurry, and sat on the bench to discuss the merits of chard, he asked if we'd ever set potatoes called Tibets. 'No', said Wilf. 'Right so', said the man, 'I'll be passing tomorrow in the car and I'll throw in a few for you there in the boot.'

And he did. Somewhere round lunchtime the following day, he arrived with a bag of potatoes for eating, another for seed, and an armful of leeks for good measure.

Checked out on the Internet, the Tibets turned out to be an old blight-resistant strain. Wilf set them the following year alongside our Champions and we sat back to see what would happen. It was a bad year for harvests of every kind. Wet, muggy weather blighted the Champions and sent slugs chomping happily through our greens. But the Tibets were triumphant, that year and each year since; as I'm typing this their purple flowers and green-leaved stalks are waving in the wind outside my window, and Wilf has just dug a pot of spuds for dinner.

If you look up 'kitchen' in a dictionary you're unlikely to find it defined as 'a side dish used to flavour a meal of potatoes'. But, in living memory, that was what the word meant here in rural Ireland. In the Irish Folklore Commission's archive there's a beautifully observed pen-and-ink drawing called *Ag ithe na preataí* (Egg ih-heh nah praw-tee) which means 'eating the potatoes'. Made in 1949 by an artist called Simon Coleman, it shows a family sitting round a basket of boiled potatoes balanced on a churn. They're dipping them into a dish of salt herring set in the centre of the basket, which itself would have been used to strain off the water in which the spuds had been boiled.

The old people here knew that a dish of 'kitchen' can turn a pot of home-grown potatoes into a feast. The possibilities are endless. Try sliced roasted beetroot dressed with vinegar and fresh thyme; yoghurt or buttermilk flavoured with onion; salt fish; or even just mayonnaise or grated cheese.

This is a month for turning fruits and vegetables from the garden into jams and chutneys for the store cupboard. But as summer work winds down and friends have time to drop by unexpectedly again, there's music by the fire too, and pauses for cups of tea on the bench by the door.

Early Irish poetry was intended to be heard, not read, and it may have been usual to hear it with musical accompaniment. From the Middle Ages to the eighteenth century some travelling poet-harpists performed their own tunes and lyrics, often in praise of local chieftains or commemorating historic events. These days verses and songs are still made about local heroes or called after a specific place or occasion.

Since we've lived here in Neillí's house Wilf has occasionally composed a jig or a polka for particular events, such as friends' birthdays. True to his classical tradition, he writes them down. And, true to the native Irish tradition, if one of them happens to be passed on, it has always been picked up by ear.

Dried rosemary
and lavender
preserve summer
flavours and
scents.

In Ireland apple tarts are traditionally flavoured with cloves. I make mine with rich shortcrust pastry. Sieve 125 g plain four and a pinch of salt into a large bowl. Rub in 60 g cold butter and 25 g hard white fat till it looks like fine breadcrumbs, then stir in a teaspoonful of caster sugar. Add about 2 tsps of water to an egg yolk and cut the wet ingredients into the dry ones with a knife. When it comes together in a ball, rest it in the fridge for about 30 mins.

Toss chopped apples over a low heat in a little butter with a couple of cloves and a handful of sultanas, to release the juice of the fruit and the flavour of the spice.

Roll out your pastry lid, tuck it over your filling in a shallow pie plate, cut slits to release the steam and bake at 200 °C for about 15 mins.

This tree was in the garden when we came here. They're dessert apples, very crunchy but not particularly sweet; I think they must have been bred mainly for their red colour which is spectacular in September. They store well in the cool, dark shed, and keep their texture and skin colour when cooked. I often put them in tarts instead of using cooking apples like Bramleys.

One of the most significant turning points in the Celtic calendar takes place about 23 September. It's the autumn equinox after which, in the northern hemisphere, the arc of the sun across the sky each day starts to shift towards the south. Migratory birds and butterflies follow the sun's southerly path while small mammals, like hedgehogs, prepare to hibernate. Other wild animals, like the hare which grazes on grass and herbs throughout the year, require biodiversity in the native landscape for survival. As the days and nights grow colder they're grateful for slightly unkempt, chemical-free gardens like ours to forage in.

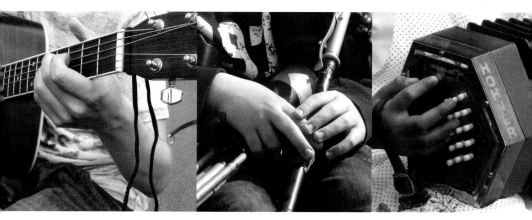

Honeybees depend on instinctive communal action to make it through the coming months. As temperatures drop, the bees form a cluster within their hive and regularly change places from the circumference to the centre, so that each keeps warm and has opportunities to walk around over the comb and eat honey.

I love the way that, like the bees, human communities here draw together and become more interdependent in the face of the cold months to come. September begins the nights by the fire when customs and skills are passed on.

OCTOBER

The Third Month of Lughnasa

In this last month of their calendar, on the night we now call Halloween, the ancient Celts celebrated the constant stream of energy which, in their world view, animates the universe.

At this time of year the colours of the landscape here are muted. In the garden fennel flowers powder away in drifts of yellow dust leaving silver seed pods on bleached stalks like bones. The dead stalks pull easily from the earth and their faint, spicy smell mixes with the rich smell of black turf when they're thrown on the fire.

By the roadsides the neon colours of summer fuchsia and montbretia give way to the browns and greys of the older, native foliage.

In the high fields the bony spine of the peninsula's central mountain range rears up through grass melted by the rain. And voices speak from weathered stones.

One day, only a few years ago, a Dingle man called Colm Banbury was guiding two tourists on a walk up Mount Brandon. It's a route he knows well and had walked many times before. But on that day, by sheer chance, he looked down and there, low to the ground on a rock slab, he saw something he hadn't noticed before. It was a perfectly carved spiral.

Etched on a rock high above the ocean, patched with moss and lichen and half-hidden by heather and furze, it echoes examples of Megalithic art which are found all across the world.

Across continents and millennia, human beings have always shared one central reason for telling stories and making pictures. They are ways of expressing, communicating and trying to understand the purpose and complexity of life. Like many ancient peoples worldwide, the Celts here in Ireland appear to have made no images of their fertility goddess in human form. They imagined her as a woman and indicated her attributes by associating her in stories with bees, flowers, fertility and the earth itself. But, essentially, she was an abstract expression of a sophisticated world view which fuses our modern ideas of art, science, religion, medicine and psychology into a dynamic whole.

For the ancient Celts, to whom Mount Brandon was holy, the Goddess was both memory and potential. The spiral symbol with which their artists described her was an expression of the idea of eternity.

Irish Soda Bread

Ingredients

350 g plain white unbleached flour
115 g wholemeal flour
A level tsp of bicarbonate soda
360 ml sour milk or buttermilk

Method

1. Sieve dry ingredients into a big bowl. Make a well in the centre. Pour in the milk and, using one hand and turning the bowl with the other, mix the ingredients together from the outside to the centre. You want a soft, not sticky dough, so add a handful of wholemeal flour if you need to, and bring it all together as quickly as possible.

2. Knead very briefly on a floured board, just to make a ball. Flatten slightly with your hand and cut a cross through it. (You can go almost right through because it'll come together a lot when it rises.)

3. Bake on a heavy, floured baking sheet for 15 mins at 230 °C. Then reduce the heat to 200 °C for about another 15 mins.

4. It's done when it sounds hollow when you tap the base. Cool on a wire rack.

Best on the day you bake it, I find it's grand the next day too, provided you keep it in an airtight container.

One thing I know for certain is that life is joined up in ways that our ancestors, even only few generations back, were better placed to recognise than we are. Twenty-first-century living is increasingly driven by the idea that everything desirable has to be purchased, and that everything thing we buy must be the best, the fastest, the newest and the most exciting product available. Then, as soon as we do buy something, we're encouraged to despise what we have and reject it for something deemed better. In the midst of this bombardment it's hard to appreciate silence, patience, repeated rhythms, and the ways in which relationships between material, intellectual, emotional and spiritual things are central to well-being and health.

Here in Neillí's house I'm learning to shift my perspective in ways so small that they can seem foolish. But for me they make a difference. I'm finding that recipes don't always have to be exact, that each food springs from the earth in its season, and that it's possible for enough to be plenty. I've realised that the shape of my working day doesn't have to be rigid: though deadlines have to be met, I allow myself to respond to the weather, or to the fact that a neighbour needs help or drops in for a chat.

Most of all I'm beginning to recognise my place in a bigger picture. Growing, ripening and withering are part of an inevitable, cyclical process, and while I move steadily towards my own withering the universe around me is pulsing with life.

Looking back through the photos in this book, I'm struck by how often I've used pictures of bees and of hands. That wasn't planned. To my eye, hands are always interesting. They are dynamic, expressive and creative and I love how, even in isolation, they can carry a clear sense of purpose or emotion. But, looking at where I've placed the photos in this book, I can see that they've emerged here as a metaphor for Corca Dhuibhne's tradition of handing on its inherited culture and customs.

Bees are pollinators. As they gather nectar, a concentrated energy source, and pollen, a high-protein food, they transfer pollen from the male anthers to the female stigma of flowers. They're beautiful and hard for a photographer to catch, which is partly why I keep trying to photograph them. But because an earth with no pollinators would no longer produce food, they're also associated with the fertility goddess Danú, whose presence is embedded in the name of Corca Dhuibhne.

I didn't start this book from metaphor, or from the way that awareness of bees and hands prompts mindfulness of individuality and community and the relationship between them. But that, it appears, is where I've ended up.

From the end of the twentieth century, insect, bird and animal pollinators and wild bees have declined, and many pollinator species worldwide are now in danger of extinction. Two years ago a neighbour of ours, a beekeeper, visited his hives and found his bees were dead. After a while he bought two new queens, hoping to build up a new bee population in his empty hives. But those queens died as well. Disappointed, he stopped trying.

Then, a few weeks ago, he noticed honeybees on the old beelines across his garden, carrying pollen. Without his having done anything at all, a new queen and her bees had moved in to one of his beehives. This is one of the photos that Wilf and I took of them the other day. We didn't stay long, the bees were troubled by our presence and their work was more important than ours.

I don't know why pollinators are declining. What I do know is that scientists have begun to publish evidence that supports the ancient principle that the earth itself is a living organism and that all life interacts and is interdependent. At the same time, indigenous leaders worldwide say that many 21st-century ecological programmes are disruptive of systems far more complex than our science can measure. I think we need to listen to them.

This has been a book about ordinary things and small, bright pleasures that can easily go unnoticed. You can find them anywhere.

I think the reason I've found them at the end of the Dingle peninsula is partly that my life here encourages awareness. Here the living rhythms of an ancient oral culture inform the modern world of Twitter and Facebook. The dominating presence of Mount Brandon, and the particular quality of the light reflected off the ocean, throw scale and specificity into focus, setting human life into context. I walk on the beaches or the hills and I'm shattered by silence.

Most of all, I marvel at the language. Though my Irish is relatively fluent, I wasn't raised thinking in it, and that makes a difference. As my mind moves from Irish to English and back again, I realise how deeply concepts and ideas are affected by environment. People here think in a language which reflects a profound awareness of nature and of the cycle of the seasons. There's a stretch in the March days that's the length of a cockerel's footstep. July is 'the hungry month'. The sky god's name is embedded in the Irish word for August. And the Wran, or Wren's, Day preserves echoes of midwinter rites that stretch back across millennia to a powerful belief in a living universe animated by a single, shared spirit.

Set against that vast, vibrant world view, the twist of a tune, the weight of a well-made spade, or the taste of water may seem unimportant. Yet in such a world view nothing is, or can be, unimportant. All that exists is contained in all other things, and the small things are entry points to recognition of the whole: the flour between your fingers, the swirl of your hand as you draw in the buttermilk, the bowl you choose to mix it in, and the strength of the flame that causes your bread to rise.